YOUR COMPANION
THROUGH
ADDICTION

CHAPTERS BY JAMES HIGHTOWER
DEVOTIONS BY PETER FERGUSON

OUT OF
THE DEPTHS

Abingdon Press

Nashville

OUT OF THE DEPTHS:
YOUR COMPANION THROUGH ADDICTION

Copyright © 2018 by Abingdon Press

This book is printed on acid-free paper.

978-1-5018-7132-0

18 19 20 21 22 23 24 25 26 27—10 9 8 7 6 5 4 3 2 1
MANUFACTURED IN THE UNITED STATES OF AMERICA

CONTENTS

INTRODUCTION

Today you only have to read the newsfeed on your phone, watch the news or reality shows on television, or listen to the radio to know how pervasive substance abuse is, not only in the US but worldwide. The story of addiction becomes much more real for most of us because of our personal stories of addiction. Whether we suffer from an addiction or not, nearly everyone's life is touched by the addiction of a relative or friend. We know the monster of addiction can be deadly. This is a crisis of epidemic proportions, and it is growing.

Still, there is hope, and you are holding a small symbol of it in your hand. Whether it is your addiction or that of a loved one that has caused you to read this little book, we thank you for allowing us to walk with you on this journey of self-exploration and pray that, if need be, you may—perhaps—experience a change in attitude or habits. In these pages, you will find helpful information about addiction and honest and faithful words about the journey through it. Some of the stories may resonate with you; others will not. Take what works for you and leave the rest. And remember, you are not alone. We are honored to serve as your companions through addiction.

Grace and peace,
James Hightower & Peter Ferguson

Chapter One

UNDERSTANDING & RECOGNIZING ADDICTION

WHAT IS ADDICTION?

If you have attempted to stop drinking, using drugs, or engaging in other addictive behaviors without help (or even with help!), you know how difficult it can be. By this time you may believe you are weak and be haunted by thoughts like, "If I were only stronger I could beat this thing." You may believe by now you just come from "bad seed" and are cursed to lose your health, family, financial security, standing in the community, and more. The shame cycle of addiction can be crushing.

Let's be clear: addiction is not about being weak or immoral. You *may* have disregarded your families, friends, and responsibilities in service to your addiction. You *may* have lied to keep the addiction going. You *may* have done some really bad things to acquire the drugs you are addicted to. You *may* have compromised your own moral compass in your addiction. You *may* even have robbed or sold your body just to get the fix your body was telling you it needed. Doing bad things does not make you a bad person.

Addiction is a brain disease. The nature of this brain disease is that the addiction to particular drug(s) or behavior(s) takes over your life, becoming your focus throughout each day. The addiction becomes more important than your partner, children, extended family, work, or reputation. It involves compulsive behavior that is incredibly hard to control. You do things you never thought you would or that you don't know why you are doing. The nature of addiction kicks the addicted person's self-esteem into the gutter. But you (or your loved one) is more than your (or their) addiction. You (and they) are a beloved child of God who suffers from a particular kind of illness. That doesn't make you any less loved or lovable.

When addicted, your brain and body become dependent on a certain substance and the chemical release associated with its ingestion or consumption. As your body becomes used to and then dependent on these chemicals, it needs more and more to achieve the same high, thus fueling the cycle of addiction. With many substances, once your body because accustomed to them, it becomes unable to function properly without them, triggering physical withdrawal symptoms such as shakes

It is also possible to be addicted to a behavior or set of behaviors. Such addictions are called "process addictions." For the first time, in the recent 5th Edition of the *Diagnostic and Statistical Manual*, gambling is listed as an addictive disorder.[1] The essential quality of the addiction is that the gambling is uncontrolled and like the other addictions makes life unmanageable. Other process addictions include (but are not limited to) eating disorders, self-harm/cutting, pornography, and compulsive shopping.

THE ADDICTIVE PERSONALITY

Over the years of working with people who are addicted to a substance or activity and in working with my own addictive tendencies, I have found several personality traits that are characteristic of persons with addictions. Of course, not everyone who becomes addicted displays these traits, but they are more common in the addicted population.

Low self-esteem: Feeling inadequate is a common human experience. Getting through day-to-day life can be especially difficult when you have trouble thinking of yourself as worthy of love and success. Many people use coping skills to overcome this gap, but with an addicted personality, turning to drugs and/or alcohol becomes the easy way out. One of the miracles of 12-Step programs is learning to "live life on life's terms" rather than taking the easy way out.

Though it is somewhat counter-intuitive, low self-esteem can also manifest itself as narcissism. Narcissists believe, usually unconsciously, that they can protect themselves from feelings of low self-esteem by acting as if (and attempting to convince themselves and those around them that) they are the center of the universe.

All-or-nothing thinking: People prone to addiction tend to think in black and white terms, with little tolerance for gray or ambiguity.

Thinking or talking in extreme terms limits the broad experience of emotions and possibility. Very rarely is anything (or anyone) "all good" or "all bad." Lack of nuanced thinking or emotions can lead to hopelessness, resignation, intolerance, and an inability to tolerate distress.

Inability to deal with stress: Being human is hard. Life is demanding. For people who have a difficult time dealing with stress, drugs and alcohol become a coping mechanism. If the stressed-out person zones out then the stress goes away…until they sober up. Most addictive behaviors serve a numbing purpose. The inability to deal with stress (or distress) often leads to compulsive behavior.

Inability to delay gratification: The addicted person becomes angry when needs (real or perceived) are not met immediately. Not being able to delay gratification can lead to making poor choices to serve our short-term desires without regard for our long-term needs. While "good things come to those who wait," our society and the addicted personality have a hard time waiting.

Isolation: The deep loneliness of isolation can stem from situational reality or a fear of being social. This trait can run from anxiety in a social situation (thus making one afraid to interact) to a learned withdrawal due to lack of safety, to being antisocial. This antisocial aspect may stem from not conforming to society's ideal standards, past traumatic experiences, social anxiety, or a multitude of other factors.

Resentment: Taken together, these characteristics can generate a lot of anger. Addicts often have a difficult time handling or resolving anger in a healthy manner. This buried anger easily becomes resentment. Resentment overrides our rational mind and amplifies every slight we feel, real or perceived.

You may be thinking to yourself, "I have every one of those characteristics; am I in trouble?" Not necessarily. Many people who live somewhere on the spectrum of these personality traits never become addicted. Some do. These traits are not determinants of addiction, but determinants of the *likelihood* of addiction.

People with addictive personalities often fall victim to multiple forms of addiction. When an addicted person begins to stop one addictive behavior, it is easy to transition to another addiction. This process is called cross addiction, replacing one substance or behavior for another that gives a similar feeling as what you have been used to. A person may go from abusing alcohol to abusing prescription drugs or from an opioid addiction to gambling addiction. This tendency is also called "urge surfing." The urge is still there; the way to mollify it has changed. To truly move into recovery, the urges themselves must be addressed.

If you have an addictive personality and you are addicted to a substance, caution is advised. You are likely to be at a higher than normal risk of becoming addicted to another substance or behavior.

Many addicts carry a dual diagnosis, meaning that they have a psychiatric diagnosis separate from the diagnosis of substance abuse. A person may have anxiety or depression. Or a person may have a diagnosis of bipolar disorder or schizophrenia alongside the diagnosis of substance abuse. Often the addiction has developed as a way of coping with or self-medicating for the underlying disorder. If a person has a dual diagnosis, which is highly likely, then being attentive to how the issues interface with one another is very important for you and your doctor. Having a frank discussion with your medical team about your drug/behavior of choice and your history of addiction will help your medical team prescribe appropriate medications to maximize your success in recovery. (For example, someone with an anxiety disorder who has a history of abusing sedatives should only be prescribed sedatives under very close supervision, if at all.)

Do not be afraid, ashamed, or embarrassed to be honest with your care providers. Your goal (and theirs!) is a successful and sustained recovery. Moving into recovery requires honesty both with the people around you and yourself. It is impossible to get better without owning that you have a problem. Still, it is easy to deny your history or your problem. If you hear yourself saying things like, "If I can go three days without shooting up, then I'm okay," or, "I can control my drinking or drugging by using scotch rather than whiskey," you are likely going to return to the same self-abusive behaviors. But how do you know if you are in denial? How can you tell if you are addicted?

AM I ADDICTED?

By this time, you have several questions to answer. I encourage you to use the "rigorous honesty" encouraged in Alcoholic Anonymous and other treatment programs as you answer these questions:

1. Do you crave a drug that is either a depressant or stimulant? Do you crave the release or rush of engaging in a particular behavior?

2. Do you have a drug or behavior of choice?

3. Is the drug you are currently taking or behavior you are engaging in your drug/behavior of choice? Do you find yourself urge surfing?

4. Are you physically dependent on a high from drugs or addictive behaviors? The clearest way to answer is to ask yourself, "Do I ingest enough drug to change my physical, mental, emotional and/or spiritual condition?" When you stop the drug/behavior do you have withdrawal symptoms that are physical, mental, emotional and/or spiritual?

5. Do you have a continued need for the high even though it is giving you physical, mental, emotional, or spiritual problems?

6. Does your drug or behavior use cause interpersonal problems with family, friends, co-workers, or others?

7. Does your use interfere with your work (paid, volunteer, or within the family)?

8. Has your drug or behavior use caused encounters with the criminal justice system or medical establishment? Examples of this could be driving under the influence; arrest for possessing, selling, buying, or attempting to buy illicit drugs; public intoxication; or illicit actions in the service of obtaining drugs (burglary or prostitution). Have you been banned from certain doctors' offices or emergency rooms as a "frequent flyer" for pain meds? Have you gambled money that was not yours?

If you consult a mental health worker or medical professional concerning your possible addiction, they can be expected to ask certain questions about your drug use or behaviors.

1.   What type of drug/behaviors do you use?

2.   What is your specific drug/behavior of choice?

3.   How much do you use?

4.   How often do you use?

5.   For how long you have been using?

6.   If you have attempted to stop, what have you done?

7.   How long did it work and what withdrawal symptoms did you have?

8.   How many times have you attempted to stop?

The medical or mental health professional will also want to know about difficulties you have had that have been a direct effect of drug or behavior use: relationship issues such as a partner threating to leave or having left you, occupational issues such as job loss or being sent to treatment as a qualification to return to work, encounters with the law (tickets, house arrest, incarceration, drug court), etc.

Now is the time to ask, based on all the information above, "Am I addicted?" Being honest with yourself in this moment can be terrifying, but it can also be extremely liberating.

Chapter Two

APPROACHES TO TREATMENT & RECOVERY

I f you have come to believe an addictive substance or behavior is interfering with your living a full and contented life, I invite you to continue reading. If you have decided you want recovery and you will do anything to get it, or even if you are willing to entertain the notion, I am going to give you as much help as I can to get you successfully started toward recovery.

The initial question to answer is which type(s) of help is most appropriate for you. If you don't know who to contact for help, your best bet may be to start with your doctor. He or she can help you understand your options and connect you with a therapist and/or treatment facility or group. Several options are described below. Many addicts will participate in a combination of these treatment modalities in their recovery journey.

Individual counseling: Most often individual counseling helps you learn what intrapsychic pain led to the addiction. Since each of our stories are unique, this time of discovery will be about your journey and when you went from firm ground (if it ever was) to the quicksand of addiction.

Your individual counseling will also assess for any co-occurring disorders such as depression, anxiety, other addictions, etc. The counselor will make referrals as appropriate to physicians for medication, clergy for the spiritual aspect of recovery, local support groups, or vocational rehabilitation for regional resources in job preparedness. Counselors often suggest you become involved in Alcoholics Anonymous, Narcotics Anonymous, Sex Addicts Anonymous, or another group so that you are in a program of recovery.

Individual counselors use a wide variety of counseling theories to help people. However, with substance abuse issues (as well as mood disorders such as anxiety and depression) cognitive behavioral therapy is often used. This therapy helps combat negative thoughts by recognizing and stopping negative patterns of thinking or behaving. A negative thought might be, "I am so lonely now that I can't go out to the bars with my friends anymore." To change that thought pattern, you might say to yourself, "I am so glad when I wake up in the morning I will know what I said last night" or, "I'm thankful I will not have to search for my car tomorrow morning," or even, "I can still go out to dinner with a friend, and I won't have to worry about blue-lights flashing behind my vehicle on the way home." Dialectical behavior therapy (DBT) is a specific kind of cognitive behavioral therapy emphasizing skill development in mindfulness, distress tolerance, emotional regulation, and interpersonal effectiveness.

Group counseling: Group counseling is often used in conjunction with individual counseling. Group counseling, also known as group therapy, is facilitated by one or two trained mental health workers. The advantages of group counseling including learning that you are not alone in your story, developing deep trust within a group or between group members, and a experiencing a sense of belonging to combat the isolation that fuels addiction.

Being aware that other people have felt what you are feeling now can also validate what you are feeling. This, again, has the potential to reduce the sense of isolation that so often occurs with addiction, particularly the later stages of the disease. Group members share the journey and hold each other accountable. Group counseling costs less than individual counseling, so it may be more accessible and sustainable for some people.

Inpatient treatment: In-hospital treatment beyond three to seven days of medically supervised detox is rare, mostly due to insurance and financial issues. Inpatient treatment for co-occurring issues such as depression or schizophrenia, however, is more common, though it, as well, often spans just a few days. Inpatient treatment takes place in a behavioral care hospital, a behavioral care unit within a hospital (many Veteran Administration hospitals have a substance abuse unit), or an inpatient specialty hospital that focuses on addiction.

Residential treatment: This type of treatment is commonly known as "rehab." The length of stay is most often thirty to ninety days. There may be an intake period, such as detoxing or re-feeding treatment when dealing with eating disorders. Rehab will also include addiction education, medication management, individual counseling, group counseling, family counseling, follow-up care, and, depending on the facility, 12-Step meetings. Your treatment facility will also help you set up continuing care, known as "aftercare," often involving individual, group counseling, and family counseling.

If you don't know where to start, you can find rehab or recovery treatment facilities near you by searching on the web. You will likely have many results come up. The ease of finding a rehab center shows the enormity of the problem of addiction. If possible, take care to research different approaches and specialties of different facilities so you can find one that will be most useful on your journey. Quality of treatment facilities vary widely; if possible, seek out recommendations from your doctor, therapist, pastor, or other caring professional. Do not, however, let not finding the perfect facility keep you or your family member from entering treatment.

Partial hospitalization programs: This level of treatment is not an inpatient hospitalization, though it is sometimes held at a hospital. Nonetheless this is intensive treatment which you attend multiple times a week for most of the day. It is sometimes referred to as day treatment. It is imperative that a person be stabilized enough to benefit from this type of treatment, given the freedom that such structure allows outside of treatment hours. In partial hospitalization treatment you can expect to spend the day in treatment and return home in the evening. You will have individual counseling, group counseling, family counseling, and education about addiction, coping skills, and relapse prevention. You will also begin to make plans for aftercare or your next steps in recovery treatment. Partial hospitalization programs will often be able to treat dual diagnosis such as PTSD, anxiety, or bipolar disorder, and multiple addictions.

Intensive outpatient treatment: This form of treatment means several times a week for a few hours at a time. It is often chosen for its flexibility for people who have to work or do not have insurance coverage for the higher levels of care or those who are "stepping down" from higher levels of treatment. Outpatient treatment is not suitable for those who are severely addicted or those who fear relapse if not in an inpatient, residential, or partial hospitalization treatment program. To succeed in intensive outpatient treatment, an individual must be highly motivated; when not under twenty-four hour care it is easy to make excuses to avoid going to evening treatment sessions and/or otherwise adhering to the program.

Twelve-step or other support groups: The 12 Steps, first outlined in the Big Book, *Alcoholics Anonymous*, in 1939, provide a process through which many people have found recovery from their addictions. Alcoholics Anonymous (AA) and its related groups are self-sustaining, peer supported, and peer run. Members of a 12-Step program are encouraged to engage a sponsor who is an addicted person in recovery to guide the "sponsee" through the 12 Steps. Regardless of you or your loved one's stage of treatment, your care team is likely to recommend 12-Step groups and "stepwork" as part of treatment.

These twelve action steps are to be courageously accomplished with a sponsor. The selection of your sponsor is up to you. In a 12-Step program no one is going to come up to you and say, "May I be your sponsor?" Taking responsibility for your work and recovery includes securing your own sponsor.

When selecting a sponsor, look for someone who has several years of sobriety, a sponsor themselves, experience in working the steps with a sponsor, a commitment to the local meeting and broader circles of your 12-Step group, clear boundaries, and a clean and joyful life. It is widely recommended in 12-Step circles that people sponsor individuals of their own sex in order to avoid the distraction of romantic entanglements. To this end, then, many LGBTQ-identifying individuals choose a sponsor who carries the lowest risk of a romantic relationship.

Since 1930 Alcoholics Anonymous has grown dramatically; AA meetings are held worldwide. In addition, the original 12 Steps have been adopted for many other groups, including Narcotics Anonymous, Gamblers Anonymous, Sexaholics Anonymous, Overeaters Anonymous, Co-dependents Anonymous, and Eating Disorders Anonymous. Many family members of addicts have found their way into their own form of recovery through Al-Anon, Alateen, Nar-anon, Adult Children of Alcoholics Anonymous, or Co-dependents Anonymous. Your family member does not need to be in recovery or working the 12 Steps in order for you to benefit from such groups; many members join as a way to cope with their loved one's active addiction.

Many, many people have found their way to sustained recovery through the structure, program, and support of the Anonymous movement. However, traditional 12-Steps groups or the original 12 Steps are not for everyone. Charlotte Kasl has developed an alternative step-work process involving 16 steps. Some of these steps parallel or echo the 12 Steps, but their intention is to empower the addict to find a path to recovery that is appropriate for them, given the particulars of their own story. For example, whereas the original 12 Steps stresses our powerlessness, Kasl's first step emphasizes finding one's own voice in order to take control back from the substance, behavior, or trauma. Such an approach can be effective for victims of trauma and historically disempowered groups, such as women.[1]

Christian recovery programs: These programs may or may not incorporate the 12 Steps, instead emphasizing biblical principles and a personal relationship with Jesus Christ to help a person in recovery. Celebrate Recovery is one such faith-based program that incorporates the 12 Steps.[2]

In residential faith-based treatment centers, living in a supportive Christian community helps the addict cut ties with the people, places, and situations that fueled their addiction. Work is often required for people in faith-based recovery programs. This helps the resident gain back a sense of dignity and positive work ethic that is often lost in addiction. Mentorship by a person who is further along in recovery is also a part of faith-based programs. Treatments plans will likely also include Bible study and regular attendance at worship. Some faith-based programs work with families so that parents or the parent affected by addiction will not be separated from their children while in recovery.

While this book is written from a Christian perspective, other treatment centers and modalities have been created for many of the world's religious perspectives.

WHICH TREATMENT OPTION IS RIGHT FOR YOU?

When choosing a treatment option and/or facility, consider the many variables at play, including availability, financial concerns, severity of addiction, dual diagnosis, and the involvement of the criminal justice system (if applicable).

Consult with your medical doctor, therapist, clergyperson, and/or your local mental health association to find out which options are available in your area, along with additional options (particularly for residential programs) that may be worth the travel. Members of the recovery community (such as your peers in AA or other support group) are generally glad to tell you about their experience in various treatment centers.

The cost of treatment varies greatly. If you have insurance (public or private, employer-based), call the number on the back or your card to inquire about coverage. They may cover certain levels of treatment and/or particular facilities. If you have the financial means to private-pay, you will have more options open to you. Some thirty-day programs can cost a thousand dollars or more a day; others may cost much less.

Severity of the addiction and what your drug of choice is will also help determine which treatment option is best for you. You may begin at one level of care, such as partial-hospitalization, only to realize that you are unable to control your use without round-the-clock monitoring, necessitating a change to a residential program. Moving between levels of care is quite common; the important part is to start somewhere and be open to the recommendations of your treatment team.

If you, like many people experiencing addiction, have a dual diagnosis (an addiction and another mental health diagnosis, such as depression or PTSD) you will need a program that treats the underlying mental health condition as well. In this case, a program with medical staff beyond the detoxification team will be helpful and, likely, essential.

If you are in the criminal justice system, the judge on your case may make the decision about placement for you. For example, you may be ordered to rehab, then house arrest, and/or drug court. Drug court is designed to keep drug-addicted offenders out of jail and in recovery. Completion of drug court can offer the incentive of having sentences dismissed, lessened, or set aside.

Finally, consider whether, given the current state of your addiction activity, you are the person best equipped to make this decision for you. It may be that it's best made by and with the people you trust most to have your best interests at heart, such as close family members or your physician. Simply put, addiction is a disease that leads to death. Where you are in your addiction may make it necessary for someone else to decide or help decide for you.

Chapter Three

SPIRITUALITY & RECOVERY

Recovery without reclaiming your own form of spirituality will be recovery found wanting. However, this subject of spirituality can be very confusing. What does it mean to be a spiritual person? And is being spiritual the same as being religious? Being spiritual is related to your human spirit; being spiritual is "soul work." When a person has developed a spirituality that works for them, there will be an integration of meaning and purpose in your life. This integrated spirituality will be evident because you will have meaning and purpose in your life. This meaning and purpose will be your lived experience because you have a sense of connectedness with yourself and others. Often, the connectedness in recovery will be a stark contrast to the isolation experienced in active addiction.

HOW DOES ADDICTION AFFECT SPIRITUALITY?

In active addiction, the lack of spirituality has markers that are easily seen by family, and friends, bosses, and co-workers. Isolation is one of these markers. Some family members report that they know their loved one is using again because they don't visit or call like they used to. Ironically, this being disconnected from others can lead to feeling abandoned. Many people, still using and in early recovery, have told me how abandoned they have felt by spouses, parents, and non-using friends. Indeed, at times this has been true. One too many calls from jail, one too many jail sentences, one too many broken promises and loved ones have let go of the relationship. I have seen people in recovery who have used up all their relationship "coins" with family or friends. But more often, I have seen families re-engage with their addicted relative when it is obvious they are working a program of recovery. Such family support can be essential.

The absence of gratitude is another marker of a lack of spirituality. If you are a user, you know that when you are in active addiction, "chasing the dime" or the next pill, drink, snort, or purge is more important than anything else. It is more important than your spouse who left you, your children that you lost to human services, or the profession you are unable to practice anymore. In contrast, a common practice in recovery communities is naming our gratitude. Being specific and naming our gratitude (as in, "I am thankful for the clean air I breathe" or "I am grateful for my family's forgiveness") can help keep us connected to the life of recovery by reminding us of what we have to lose by falling back into our addiction.

Addiction is filled with secrets. The dishonest life it necessitates is another marker of a lack of spiritual grounding. Your secret may be how many drinks you really had today. It may be how much debt you have racked up gambling. It might be how little or how much you have eaten today. You may find yourself lying to your family or boss about where you've been these past few hours or why you missed another day of work. This lifestyle of deceit eats at our self-esteem, activating large amounts of shame. Shame is a difficult emotion because shame lies to you about yourself. Shame tells you that you are bad. Shame never makes the finer point that what you are *doing* is bad and that what you do is not you. Shame is a heavy burden to bear and eventually paralyzes you. Once shame takes control of your life, you live in a state of self-loathing. Now not only are you isolated from others, but you are isolated from yourself.

Another marker of a lack of spirituality is resentment. Resentment, that internalized and unexpressed anger and disappointment that we carry around, can trigger the rebellious nature of addiction. A common saying in recovery communities is that carrying resentments around is like drinking poison and expecting the other person to die. It is neither helpful nor effective.

Resentment is closely related to forgiveness. Forgiveness is something you do for yourself; forgiveness is not about establishing a relationship with an unsafe person. It is letting go of the tightly held resentment so that *you* can heal. It is acknowledging that you have had too many drinks or too many pills over this hurt and that taking one more is one too many. The process of letting go of resentments and forgiving for your own healing is also a way of reminding yourself that this person has rented space in your head for too long. It is time to foreclose and take the space back! Carrying resentments only leads to more isolation and more shame.

This isolation from others and self-loathing leads to a shame-based life laced with fear and self-hatred. Isolation snowballs, and eventually you will likely feel isolated from God's Spirit or your understanding thereof. Addiction has become a spiritual problem; a spiritual solution is called for.

An open and honest spirituality allows the shackles of self-hatred to be broken. Shame is brought out into the light, and in the light, it withers. Dishonesty is set aside, and honestly emerges. Isolation turns to intimacy. A growing spirituality in recovery helps you be hopeful when hopelessness prevailed before. But is there only one kind of spirituality where everyone has to like the same flavor or brand? Absolutely not!

TYPES OF SPIRITUALITY

Religion is the most common type of spirituality, but it's not the only one. Organized religion is embedded in a specific expression of faith. In the Christian tradition it may be Methodist, Presbyterian, Baptist, etc., and in Judaism it may be Reformed Judaism, Orthodox Judaism, etc. Organized religion has a body of doctrine to which its adherents subscribe. These beliefs are codified in the Apostle's Creed, the Nicene Creed, and the like. Most organized religions also have a set of practices to adhere to, such as baptism, the Lord's Supper or communion, confession, private and group prayer, etc. Organized religions often have distinct beliefs about life after death and have a set of ethics by which adherents are encouraged to live. Many people have experienced recovery by digging deeper into their choice of organized religion, thus gaining a sense of purpose, meaningful relationships, and access to a power greater than themselves. Some churches even have a recovery program as a part of their ministry.

Individualized spiritual practices are another form of spirituality. These practices may or may not incorporate some forms of organized religion. You will hear a lot about mindfulness as a helpful practice in recovery and treatment circles. Mindfulness is simply practicing a non-judgmental awareness of the present moment. Living in and accepting this moment, this now, instead of ruminating over the past or worrying about the future can be life-giving to a person in recovery. Mindfulness practice promotes stress reduction and a more peaceful outlook on life. Try this exercise to begin practicing mindfulness:

> Find a comfortable seat in which you can be still. Put both feet on the floor and rest your hands on your legs. If you are comfortable doing so, close your eyes. Take a deep breath, paying attention to how the air feels coming into and moving through your body. Hold it for a moment, then exhale slowly, still drawing your attention to the feeling of your breath. Continue this intentionally slowed breathing; let your breath be your focus. When thoughts come into your mind, let them float away gently and return your focus to your breath. There's no need to judge yourself for getting distracted; our minds are trained to stay busy. Just watch your thoughts flow by like a cloud drifting through the sky. Continue this practice for two minutes, then reflect on what it was like for you? Was it easy or difficult? How do you feel now?

As you become more accustomed to practicing moments of mindfulness, you can vary the exercise, perhaps by making a scan of your body, head to toe, or taking each of your senses in turn, noting what you see, hear, feel, taste, and smell. The possibilities are endless; the point is to return your awareness to the present moment without judgment. There are also apps and podcasts that offer guided mindfulness exercises, which you can search for online.

Yoga, a Hindu spiritual practice, the use of which has spread beyond its geographic and religious heritage, focuses on breath control, meditation, and specific body postures. Yoga is excellent both to promote health and give the spiritual advantages of mindfulness meditation exercises.

Journaling is another individual spiritual practice that has great value for some people. Keeping a journal increases self-awareness and helps track your emotional highs and lows that may be connected to various events throughout your day. Journaling gives you an aerial view of your life because you can look back on how some recurring event in your life used to upset you, whereas today you have tools to respond in a different way. Journaling can be done in a variety of ways; it's not necessary that your journal be diary-like or keep track of your day-to-day goings on. Maybe people find keeping a gratitude journal helpful.

Another type of spirituality is being present in nature. As long as humans have walked this earth, we have found a walk in nature to be healing to the soul. Nature has healing properties, and sometimes just being in and appreciating the vastness of beauty of God's creation can reset your sense of being in the world. You may decide that a simple thirty-minute walk each day, a camping trip to the shore or mountains, or time planting a garden is just what the doctor ordered for your spiritual health.

The arts have offered a path to connection and healing for many people across the years. Some of the world's greatest works of art have been borne out of the pain of addiction and the attempt to connect to God out of its depths. Even if you don't consider yourself a creative person, the act of creating via visual arts, dance, words, or music can be healing and generative. In fact, some therapists specialize in art or expressive therapy. Further, you don't have to be the creator yourself to benefit from a spirituality based in art; simple enjoying art produced by others can be healing in itself, keeping your soul intact and promoting recovery.

The possibilities of spiritual practices are as varied as the people reading this book. Find your way to a spirituality that works for you. Find what connects you at your core to the source of life. That spiritual path may be your unique path, or it may be a path followed by millions. If the path you find works for you, stay on it and tweak it as needed.

THE SIGNS OF SPIRITUAL RECOVERY

Consider the following questions as a way to evaluate (without judging) your sense of spiritual recovery.

1. Do I attempt to live an honest life?

2. Am I no longer the center of the universe?

3. Do I see myself as more or less important than I am?

4. On most days and in most situations, is my courage greater than my fear?

5. Do I work at staying connected to others and to God as I understand God?

6. Is gratitude a part of my daily life?

7. Am I hopeful?

8. Do I attempt to live a life of love and justice?

9. Do I attempt to help others who can use a helping hand?

Spirituality is the cornerstone of recovery, and recovery itself can bring about a deeper, more authentic spirituality. The gifts of recovery are inextricably bound to a healthy spirituality, such as:

*   The ability to be empathetic towards others.
*   The willingness to act in behalf of others.
*   The knowledge that I am being honest.
*   The ability to be less judgmental/critical of others.
*   Having gratitude as a daily part of one's life.
*   The capacity to be less judgmental and more accepting toward myself.
*   The ability to forgive myself.
*   Accepting the past while living life today as it is, with its good and its bad.
*   Knowing a new happiness.

Recovery undoubtedly leads to a maturation of spirituality, even while spiritual development can lead you into recovery.

Chapter Four

RELAPSE PREVENTION

The technical term for staying in recovery once you get there is *relapse prevention*. Often, maintaining your recovery long-term is as hard as or harder than achieving your initial recovery. In the recovery community, you may hear people say that the problem is not stopping drinking or using; the problem is staying stopped. You must be proactive in your recovery in order to maintain it. Recovery is an ongoing action program.

In order to maintain your recovery, **take one day at a time**. Taking it twenty-four hours at a time is the only requirement. Months and years take care of themselves twenty-four hours at a time. There may be days, particularly early in your recovery, in which you have to take things one hour or one minute at a time. Break down the time into whatever increments you need in order to delay your potential use. You don't have to stay clean for your entire life today. You just have to stay clean today.

Knowing your patterns of past use can be extremely helpful. **Become aware of early signs of being triggered to drink or engage in behaviors**. Some of these triggers may revolve around certain emotions; significant life changes; common situations; or exposure to people, places, or settings related to your addicted lifestyle. Common emotional triggers include fear/anxiety, loneliness/isolation, anger, resentment, hopelessness, or even feeling overconfident in your recovery. Special care must be taken around any significant life changes, such a moving, changing jobs, or even a positive change such as getting married or having a child. Any time your body isn't functioning as fully as possible, due to hunger, fatigue, or illness (mental or physical), your risk for relapse is increased. One of the most expansive changes you will have to make in recovery is eliminating or mitigating your exposure to your former life of addiction. In order to stay healthy, it may be necessary for you to develop a new group of friends (who don't use), find new restaurants to patronize (perhaps ones without a bar), or even find new routes home (to avoid hotspots of use or purchase points). Knowing yourself—and knowing your addiction—can be your most powerful tool in maintaining recovery.

Follow the directives and advice of your treatment team. While recovery is an individual decision you must make every day (or, more likely, a series of decisions you make every day), your care team is knowledgeable and have your best interests in mind. There are times they will be in a better place to make a decision for you than you are yourself. At the same time, you must take ownership of your own behaviors and actions and be an active part of your team. Maintaining recovery means maintaining the actions that brought about recovery. Go to your therapy appointments. Follow up with your doctor. Before you step back from one form of treatment, discuss it with your team. By the time you are fully into recovery, they have likely come to know you and your addiction well and will have a helpful perspective on your recovery.

If you are in a 12-Step or other recovery support group, **work your program**. Recovering addicts have a much better relapse prevention rate if actively working their recovery program. Do your step work with your sponsor. Get a sponsor who is more than a sponsor in name only. While every sponsor works with "sponsees" differently, all effective sponsors require their sponsees to work their programs. Regularly attend your 12-Step or other support group meeting. When it becomes easy to stop or skip meetings, relapse is much more likely.

EFFECTIVELY MANAGING STRESS AND EMOTIONS

The most significant key to remaining in full recovery is learning to effectively manage your stress and emotions. Drinking, using, shopping, gambling, bingeing are all emotionally-driven behaviors; that is, we engage in them in order to avoid feeling certain emotions. Increasing your ability to manage stress and tolerate uncomfortable emotions and situations decreases your need to act out these emotionally-driven behaviors.

We all have stress. Stress can be helpful when it propels us forward (i.e., "I have an exam tomorrow; I'd better start studying"). This is "good stress" because it moves me forward and spurs me into action. On the other hand, if my anxiety about the exam makes me terrified that I will fail and flunk out of school, that stress becomes paralyzing. How we cope with stress that feels overwhelming is a central determinant of relapse and its prevention. Consider these ways of managing, even transforming, stress and anxiety.

Take care of your body. Start with the basics. Life is harder to handle if you are not taking care of your physical body. Eat a regular, healthy, and varied diet. Get enough sleep. Exercise as advised or recommended by your treatment team and under the care of your physician. Aside from the physical benefits of exercise, it can be a positive way to relieve stress, producing endorphins that help your brain shift to take a wider view of life. Taking care of your body is a way of showing compassion to yourself.

Check your thinking. In the rooms of 12-Step programs you can regularly hear people say, "I came for my drinking but stayed for my thinking." Addiction and recovery happen between our ears; addiction is a brain disease expressed in thoughts and manifested in destructive behaviors. Use CBT and DBT techniques discussed in chapter two to acknowledge and challenge negative thoughts you may have about yourself. Replace them with positive self-talk, or, on your worst days, self-talk that is at least neutral.

Express yourself. Keep a journal. The simple act of getting your negative thoughts and feelings out of mind and onto paper can have remarkable results. Seeing your thoughts in front of you can help you consider them more objectively and make connections that you might not otherwise make if the thoughts were still jumbled in your brain. In fact, a journal is sometimes called a "poor man's therapist." While journaling cannot replace a competent therapist, journaling is a great ancillary support. Even if you don't go back and analyze your thoughts, "downloading" your thoughts can be very freeing.

Find a hobby. The clearer you can be about who you are, not what you have or what you do, the better chance you will have at not relapsing. Hobbies give you a chance to explore and discover what you truly enjoy doing. You may have interests you never encountered because you have been so caught up in your addiction. A hobby also gives you the opportunity to not take yourself too seriously. Even adults need to play.

Connect with God and with other people. Participate in meditative practices, such as the mindfulness exercises described in chapter two. Guides to meditation are readily available in books and online. Yoga studios have popped up across the country. Mindfulness is a part of our larger culture. Meditative practices can be as simple as a breath prayer: pick an attribute or name for God ("Loving God,") to say on your inhale and a request or statement to say (aloud or silently) through your exhale ("hold me close). Your meditative practice can use guided imagery or relaxation techniques, moving from the top of your head to your toes, slowly relaxing your muscles.

Engage your faith community. If you have found participating in a faith community (be it a congregation, Bible study, faith-based parenting group, Celebrate Recovery, etc) to be a meaningful part of your spirituality, don't shy away from becoming—and staying—involved through your recovery.

Engage your "family of choice." We humans are born into families, created for community. As adults in recovery, we have the power to choose who we want to travel life with us. The presence of a "family of choice" (vs. your family of origin) can be a significant and positive sign of and support to a lasting recovery. When you are feeling stressed, connect with another person, whether it's your sponsor, family member, friend, or therapist, about what is stressing you and how you can handle it more positively, without using. That's a part of what a sponsor is for.

Tend to your emotional life. Learn coping and grounding skills, particularly if you, like many addicted people, have a history of trauma. Turning to an addiction is a natural, though unhealthy, way of dealing with trauma. When we have been through situations nobody should have to experience, our senses and very being are overloaded, and numbing out through our addictive behaviors can be a blessed release. Work with your therapist to develop ground techniques to keep you solidly experiencing the present moment, not reliving terrible moments of your past or being hypervigilant about future threats. One common grounding technique is cataloging your senses: what are five things, at this very moment, that you can see, hear, touch, smell, and (if applicable) taste?

Connecting with your senses necessarily grounds you in the reality of the here and now.

Monitor emotions. Feel your feelings and monitor your anger and resentments. Feelings will not dissipate until they have been fully felt. Though it sounds counterintuitive, we must dive into our emotions (without letting them control our behaviors) in order to let them go. Allow yourself to experience the highest and lowest emotions. Even though it may feel like it could kill you, nobody has ever died of a particularly unpleasant emotion. Even sadness, guilt, fear, and anger have their place in our emotional spectrum.

Learn to manage anger. Pay particular attention to how you carry your anger, as it is a common byproduct of addiction and, for many people, one of the easiest emotions to access when under stress. Anger, like other emotions, serves a purpose, namely, to tell you that a boundary has been violated. Somebody or something has crossed a line that feels significant to you. But anger also tends to be a secondary emotion, one that covers up a deeper emotion such as hurt or fear. Maybe people lash out in anger when they are unable to control a situation. Listen to your anger and let it guide you to whatever deeper, harder to access, emotion may be under the surface. Then let yourself feel that emotion. It may be helpful to practice simple anger management techniques, like pausing and counting to ten before acting on your anger so that you can be free to respond thoughtfully instead of react violently (physically or emotionally).

Feeling stress is necessary to and inherent in our survival. But as we move deeper into recovery, we learn to take life as it comes to us without immediately checking out through the use of our addictive behaviors.

CONCLUSION

What now? What's your next step?

Well, you have options. You may have already made some recovery-minded choices. Perhaps you have spoken with your doctor or other healthcare provider. Maybe you have sat in on a 12-Step meeting. Wherever you are on your path to recovery, you have choices.

The least-effective option is to do nothing. But if you continue to make that same choice, you will achieve only the same outcome. Things may even escalate and get worse. Sure, it would be amazing if you stood up and yelled, "I'm ready for recovery! Sign me up!" But you don't have to show such confidence just yet. All you need to do right now is to take the next right step. Call your doctor. Make an appointment with a therapist. Talk to your parent or teacher. Ask for support from your friend or pastor. Whatever that next right step is for you, gather your courage and take it. The rest will follow.

GOD, GRANT US THE SERENITY

Although versions of the Serenity Prayer have been around for many years, the one below is frequently attributed to Dr. Reinhold Niebuhr, a distinguished professor and dean at Union Theological Seminary in New York City in the 1930s. Let us consider this prayer together.

God, grant me the serenity
to accept the things I cannot change;
courage to change the things I can;
and wisdom to know the difference.

Living one day at a time;
Enjoying one moment at a time;
Accepting hardships as the pathway to peace;

Taking, as He did, this sinful world
as it is, not as I would have it;

Trusting that He will make all things right if I surrender to
    His Will;

That I may be reasonably happy in this life
and supremely happy with Him forever in the next. Amen.

As you likely know, the first several verses of this prayer have come to be known as "The Serenity Prayer," and have been central in the practice of the 12 Steps. Involved in 12 Steps or not, the simultaneous surrender and empowerment of this prayer are emblematic of our journey through addiction and into life-long recovery.

"GOD, GRANT ME THE SERENITY TO ACCEPT THE THINGS I CANNOT CHANGE"

Living life on life's terms can be very difficult. Life will throw you a miscarriage, an illness, the death of a parent, a divorce, or a layoff. At that moment you have to decide to face, or avoid facing, the life before you. For many people who suffer from addiction these life blows are cause for falling deeper into addiction. Recovery entails accepting what life throws at you rather than reacting to it through use or behaviors.

Serenity is not about being happy. You don't have to like certain life situations. But if they are out of your control, they are out of your control. The serenity comes when you let go of that which you cannot control, that which you cannot change. Often people with addiction issues find it virtually impossible to face what life brings because fear is overwhelming. The response to the fear is to try to control everything and everyone within your reach. In recovery we learn that this attempt to control never works.

"COURAGE TO CHANGE THE THINGS I CAN"

Knowing when to act is essential. If a loved one is dying you cannot change the impending death. But what can you change? You can change your reaction. Instead of choosing to drink or get high to avoid feeling your grief, you can call your sponsor, go to a meeting, or connect or reconnect with family members. You can eat healthily and rest. You can pray or meditate. You can spend whatever time you have left with your loved one fully present, instead of hiding yourself in the numbness of your addiction.

The possibility for change is endless. But old habits, old responses die hard. Sometimes it can be difficult to imagine another way of responding. The courage to change your old way of responding is a huge change. But you can do it. Just don't pick up that next drink or drug. That takes courage.

"AND WISDOM TO KNOW THE DIFFERENCE"

Knowing what you have to accept and what you can change takes wisdom. Use the tools acquired through your recovery program to help you discern what is yours to change and what is not. The wisest choice may be to ask for help. That help may come from God, your sponsor, a friend in the program, your church friends, or your pastor. In recovery you become humble enough to ask for help.

You are only asked to do recovery one day at a time. No one has more than a twenty-four-hour reprieve. Sometimes, particularly in early recovery, it is only one moment at a time, as we have discussed.

This prayer highlights the hope embedded in Christianity. While Jesus died on the cross, death didn't have the final word. In Jesus's resurrection we experience the all-encompassing, all-powerful love of the creator of the universe. Death did not have the final word in Jesus Christ; addiction will not have the final word in your story.

As the author of Psalm 130 (from which this book series takes its name) cried from "out of the depths," you too may be at a low point in your life (v. 1 NRSV). This may be your rock bottom. You may not feel any sense of hope. But neither did Jesus's disciples that Saturday after he died. And yet, God's love won the day. Because of our faith—or, more specifically, because of God's love for us—we have hope. Even while in the depths, we can continue to pray with the psalmist: "O Israel, hope in the Lord! For with the Lord there is steadfast love, and with him is great power to redeem" (v. 7 NRSV). There is hope for you, for your loved one, for each of us, yet.

THE GIFT OF TRUTH

Then you will know the truth, and the truth will set you free.
—John 8:32

My wife had told me for years that I had a problem with drinking. Each time she brought it up we would argue. I like to argue. I want not only to win the argument but also conquer the foe, which usually resulted in my wife crying and locking me out of our room. I tried to convince her that she was the problem—she was crazy. I drink a few beers, no big deal. I was fine.

We ended up going to marriage counseling and then individual counseling. In one of my individual sessions we talked about how my wife was always nagging me; wouldn't my life be so much better if she left me alone? The therapist had a novel idea: what if I took an alcoholism inventory? We could find out the truth once and for all. The results were disheartening. I drank—and acted—like an alcoholic.

This new information cracked my previously impenetrable wall of defense and denial. I knew in my heart that I was an alcoholic. I did not want to spend the rest of my life obsessed with drinking, yet I could not envision life without it, either.

Personal growth comes slow for me. But I recognize now that this therapy session was a turning point. I did not accept this gift of awareness right away; it took me a few more months of misery before I got help. I knew people around me were telling me the truth because they loved me, but it took time before I loved myself enough to seek God and ask for help.

God, please open me up to hear and receive the truth. Amen.

EXPERIENCING GOD

Create a clean heart for me, God; put a new, faithful spirit deep inside me!
—Psalm 51:10

As a pastor's kid, I have been in church all my life. It was hard listening to my dad preach every Sunday. The same voice that yelled at me spoke from the pulpit as the voice of God. I'm not sure if it is ironic or sad that I became a pastor. My years of drinking and drugs were hard on my family (and on me), so when I heard a "calling" to ministry, everyone was so proud.

Through my first few years of ministry, I was sober. When I was in my second year of seminary, though, I started drinking again. I went to an Episcopal seminary where real wine (instead of grape juice) was served at communion. I thought it was no big deal, but it actually led to me having a taste for alcohol again.

When I entered treatment and realized that recovery is a spiritual process, I thought, "No problem!" Then I started to listen. There were people in that room who were not lifelong church members; they did not go to seminary, but they knew God more deeply and personally than I ever had.

I came to realize that what I thought I knew about God got in the way of my experience of God. I set out to be open to a new understanding of God in Jesus Christ. Because of this openness, I have a much different relationship with Jesus today.

My lack of an intimate, personal faith is not the church's fault. I learned in recovery that I had lived an intellectual faith, not one grounded in love and action. God is in the loving and in the acting.

God, let me forget what I think I know of you so that I may have a fresh experience of you. Amen.

IN HIDING

God said that light should shine out of the darkness. He is the same one who shone in our hearts to give us the light of the knowledge of God's glory in the face of Jesus Christ.

—2 Corinthians 4:6

I have been afraid of life as long as I can remember.

I have endlessly sought ways to find comfort or safety to calm my fears. TV and food were my first comforts. I loved anything from potato chips to Pizza Hut. I would make rituals out of my eating and entertainment. It took extensive planning to make sure all the food was prepared by the time my TV show started. As I got older I discovered that both running and Jesus could provide a momentary release from my fears. But nothing worked better than alcohol and drugs. I could drink all day or smoke marijuana from my first breath of the day to my last. I would call it my "cave time."

In the "cave," I was safe from all the scary things that existed in the world. I would turn off my phone, lock my doors, and do nothing but seek comfort. It was hard for me to exist outside of the cave. My loved ones, even, felt like too much and I had to shut them out. Our relationships suffered tremendously. Looking back, I give myself grace about that time in my life. I cannot help how I was wired. I could not stop the fear from consuming my life.

I still have times when I long to be in the cave. But I have also learned that fear is not a lack of faith; fear is an opportunity to seek God. I know that without God I cannot face life. Fear does not have to be my enemy now, because I can look fear in the eye and know that Jesus is there with me. I am no longer a little boy alone in the dark.

Jesus, I know you are with me in my fears and dark times. Open me up to take comfort in your presence. Amen.

OUT OF CONTROL

But God chose what the world considers foolish to shame the wise. God chose what the world considers weak to shame the strong.
—*1 Corinthians 1:27*

I was told early in recovery that, at some point, I had to admit that I was powerless over alcohol. The idea of powerlessness was revolting. I flat-out did not believe it. I began to accept my powerlessness when my sponsor showed me the cycle of addiction. It says that we go on a spree, experience remorse, and then resolve to quit for good. I knew what that looked like in my life.

I would drink 10–15 beers [spree]. I would wake up or sober up feeling disgusted with myself and guilty that I got drunk again [remorse]. I then resolved that today I would stay sober. I began feeling better, but when it got to be around five o'clock, the idea of a cold beer sounded nice. The idea of not feeling anything for a few hours sounded nice. Before I knew what I was doing, I was six beers deep, knowing that I would not stop until I passed out. This cycle of spree, remorse, and resolve repeated itself almost every day, no matter how hard I tried to stop. I was powerless to break the cycle.

I needed God to do for me what I could not or would not do for myself. When I asked for help, God provided the power that I did not have to stop drinking. It was because of a loving God that I don't have to live that cycle anymore. I am free.

◇◇◇◇◇◇◇◇◇◇◇◇◇◇◇◇◇◇◇◇◇◇◇◇◇◇◇◇◇◇◇◇◇◇◇◇◇◇

God, do for me what I cannot or will not do for myself. Amen.

◇◇◇◇◇◇◇◇◇◇◇◇◇◇◇◇◇◇◇◇◇◇◇◇◇◇◇◇◇◇◇◇◇◇◇◇◇◇

FEELINGS

Look at my suffering and trouble—forgive all my sins!
—Psalm 25:18

When I was in treatment, we would sit in a circle looking at a list of feelings. The facilitator would ask me, "Peter, how does that make you feel?" I would look down at the list of eight feelings with great confusion. I had no idea what I was feeling. In my childhood, we could only experience two emotions: rage and sadness, both of which had to be pushed down and ignored.

Eventually, I learned that in me, fear leads to anger. I would get angry when I was afraid that I would either lose something that I had or not get something that I wanted. Rage came out when I got really fearful and had to get "big," either verbally or physically, to get my way. I also rejected loneliness and sadness, which seemed pathetic. They were two more normal expressions of humanity that I refused to experience.

My inability to sit with emotions fed my addictive behaviors. When I was fearful and lonely I refused to feel either emotion. They were uncomfortable. This discomfort was intolerable and unacceptable, so I needed something to make me feel better (such as porn, food, alcohol, or praise). I have discovered that when I name my feelings and allow myself to feel them, they dissipate. The feelings no longer stir inside of me, making me uncomfortable, so I do not have to find something to make me feel better.

I also had to begin living in the world as an adult, not a little boy. A little boy is scared of big people and hides the truth out of fear of being punished. An adult tells the truth and is not afraid of being unnecessarily penalized. As long as we are not breaking the rules, the only authority we have is God—and God is love.

◇◇

God, open my ears and give voice to the truth you have placed inside me. Amen.

◇◇

THE SCARCITY MINDSET

Jesus replied, "It's written, People won't live only by bread, but by every word spoken by God."

—*Matthew 4:4*

R aised in the era of the Great Depression, my father operated out of a mindset of scarcity. He was always afraid of not having enough. His approach was wired into me, most evidently in my relationship with food.

I vividly remember the times we would go to Pizza Hut, a special treat for our family with limited financial means. I can still smell the bubbling cheese and hot pepperoni. We would always get one large thin crust pizza with pepperoni and mushrooms. A large pizza would have ten to twelve slices, depending upon who was cutting that night. So, if you do the pizza math, a family of four would have two to three slices each. As a small child that was fine, but as a teenager I would always leave the restaurant hungry.

These experiences from my childhood shaped my fear-based relationship with food. I never saw food as a way to love and fuel my body. It was always about security and comfort. When I became an adult with my own money and choices, I would order three large pizzas for our family of four. It made me feel safe that there was enough.

This fear of not having enough food has never left me, but I am beginning to know the difference between hunger and a need for safety. I try to invite God into my food choices and ask for help. I believe with God's power that I am slowly being released from the bondage of food. I no longer have the nine p.m. carb fest, but I am still scared of not having enough. I have to remind myself that, for today, my goal is progress, not perfection.

God, let me find my fulfillment and safety in you. Amen.

PEOPLE PLEASING

People tell us . . . how you turned to God from idols. As a result, you are serving the living and true God.

—*1 Thessalonians 1:9*

Is it possible to be addicted to people? Yes. It is called codependency.[1]

I had been raised a people pleaser. I believed that as long as I did everything right, everyone else would be okay. If they were okay, I would be okay. I would sacrifice my well-being out of fear of making a mistake or angering people; I didn't want to be rejected. Being alone meant that I was unworthy, defective, and unlovable—my deepest fears come true.

This codependent mindset affected how I related to myself and to others. I would not care what I ate or how I took care of my body. I would allow people to treat me without love, believing that I deserved that kind of treatment, since I was unworthy of love.

I am beginning to reverse this thinking. Today, I am less likely to spend time with toxic people. I am learning to say "No." I think about the most loving action I can take toward myself. Sometimes loving other people and myself best means not being around certain people. Other people's feelings and thoughts about me do not equate to truth; I am not stupid just because someone says or thinks I am. On the flipside, I do not have the power to make other people happy or fix them.

I am learning what loving myself really means. The more deeply I love myself, the more fully I can love God and others.

God, let me turn my life and the lives of others over to you. Amen.

STANDING STILL

I don't know what I'm doing, because I don't do what I want to do.
Instead, I do the thing that I hate.

—*Romans 7:15*

obody wants to grow up to be an addict. Little girls and boys don't play addict with their friends. It sneaks up on us. We don't think that the first time we see porn that we will become obsessed with it or that treats like ice cream (a delight to any child!) will become a struggle to set aside. We who are alcoholics see people at restaurants who inexplicably leave wine undrunk in their glass. No alcoholic leaves wine in a glass.

Are we bad people? No. Regardless of what other people in the world believe, we who suffer from addiction are not bad. We are hurting. We are scared. Things like wine, liquor, and drugs make the hurt go away and help us to feel less scared. Other people find their own ways to deal with the world—this is how we do it.

I had always tried to keep three steps ahead of my fear and pain. I would use TV, exercise, therapy, alcohol, or work in order to avoid my feelings. Recovery invites us to live life on life's terms, not our own. We face the truth instead of running from it.

After my father died, my sponsor suggested that I quit running, literally and figuratively. Stand still. Face the fear and pain, which I did. And it hurt, a lot. For weeks I would outside and sob and wail. I know this process does not sound fun, and it wasn't. But I believe it was healing. The pain was being purged from my body. Healing is rarely easy, but for me, it was a gift from God.

God, make me willing to experience your presence and healing.
Amen.

- 34 -

CLARITY

God gave them a dull spirit, so that their eyes would not see and their ears not hear, right up until the present day.

—*Romans 11:8*

A s addicts, we like to think that we know ourselves well. That way, we can rationalize and justify our behavior. The painful truth is that we cannot see ourselves clearly and, often, we are not able to admit the truth about our addictions.

In 1955, psychologists Joseph Luft and Harrington Ingham created a tool intended to measure a person's self-awareness. They called it the

JOHARI WINDOW

	Known to self	Not known to self
Known to others		
	1 Arena	3 Blindspot
Not known to others		
	2 Facade	4 Unknown

Johari Window, and it consists of four panes, each representing a different version of the self.[2]

The first pane represents the things we know about ourselves that everyone else knows also. The second pane is the things we know about ourselves that no one else knows about us. **The third pane is the things that others know about us that we don't know.** The fourth pane is a mystery. We will never fully understand ourselves or others.

We hate to admit that there is anything in our third pane. We are scared to think that we might not know everything about ourselves. Having other people know things we don't makes us vulnerable. But sometimes that knowledge of our blind spot is exactly what we need to continue in our recovery and personal growth. In recovery groups, we might say, "What we don't own owns us."

◇◇◇

God, give me sight to see myself honestly, for better and for worse.
Amen.

◇◇◇

PRACTICING TRUST

But you, Israel, trust in the LORD! God is their help and shield.
—Psalm 115:9

All of my addictions begin in the same dark place: my fear and lack of trust in God. I am afraid to surrender control, so I remain in fear. Only recently did I come to realize that I am actually addicted to my anxiety itself.

Everything, in my mind, is going to be a tragedy. The plane I am riding in is going to crash. My headache is cancer. I will soon be poor and living on the street. These panicked thoughts keep my body tense, so much so that I do have headaches or tension in my neck and shoulders. This chronic tension has led to real physical maladies that are all due to my inability to relax because of anxiety.

I have been told that, for me, anxiety is a choice. I could let go of it. But when I think about actually doing so, something in me shuts down. It's as if my body and mind are yelling, "No!" I have been anxious as long as I remember. It has been my constant companion for many years. What and who would I be without it?

I am beginning to *practice* trusting God, and practice is just practice, not perfection. I thank my anxiety for its loyalty and service. No doubt it was created to help me feel safe when I was so small and scared. Now I believe it is okay to be scared. I can be scared and still walk toward the fear, look it in the eye, and say, "Hello," instead of running or tensing up.

God, take from me any fears that keep me from loving and serving you. Amen.

APPEARANCES

So you also are complete through your union with Christ, who is the head over every ruler and authority.

—Colossians 2:10 (NLT)

I was still in active addiction while serving as a pastor. I thought I was cutting edge, a new breed of pastor who still liked to live on the wild side. The truth was I was very insecure. I had no true idea of who I was, so what I did was tried to act like people who I thought were cool. Though it's embarrassing to admit, I impersonated people who I wanted to be like.

I was lost. I did not know how to be me or stop trying to be someone else. I could not imagine a life without drinking and drugs. It was a lonely place. When people confronted me about my addictions, not only was I afraid of giving them up because I did not know how to live sober, but I did not know who I would be without them.

This is one reason why recovery programs which invite us to find a higher power are so effective. People like me find themselves through a relationship with God. For me it was a slow process; I had to first let go of the false self before I could embrace my true self. But it did happen, and today, I no longer want to be cool. I don't have to figure out who I am. I just am. At the end of the day, I am just Peter. And that is enough.

God, let me accept how you made me and let me find my true self in you. Amen.

COURAGE

Be strong and brave. Don't be afraid or lose heart!
—1 Chronicles 22:13

Walking into a 12-Step meeting was terrifying. I did not know anyone. It seemed like everyone knew each other. I felt really lonely. But I also knew if I was going to live I had to make this step. There is a saying that courage is being afraid but doing it anyway. I did it anyway.

My experience was incredible. These people were complete strangers, yet their experiences and the way they thought was so similar to mine. Now, I have never been arrested or lost my family, but the differences did not matter—when it came time to hear how they drank and the lengths they had taken to stop I found myself shaking my head yes.

My loneliness began to dissipate. I had been on a long journey to find people who understood, and there they were, sitting in a circle around me. People from different backgrounds, cultures, and economic realities were there for one purpose: to help one another stay sober.

When the subject of God, or their "higher power," came up, nobody asked each other what they thought or believe about God. There was no right or wrong way to believe. The only thing that mattered is that you found something to keep you sober. I have run into Christians that, at first, struggle with this. They have been taught that Jesus is the only way, which may be true, but if someone is staying sober and has yet to find Jesus, we celebrate the sobriety and leave it at that.

Today I am grateful for that first day that I had the courage to walk into that meeting. I am alive and living fully because I made that decision.

God, give me the courage to see sobriety and recovery. Amen.

ROCK BOTTOM

You brought up my life from the Pit, O LORD my God.
—Jonah 2:6 (NRSV)

You may have heard that an addict needs to "hit rock bottom" before they are ready to get help. This was true for me. I had countless people try to help me. They would plead for me to stop. They would try to convince me to stop by telling me how I was putting my kids, my job, and my marriage at risk. But nothing they said worked.

My experience of hitting bottom could never have been planned by anyone except for God. I had wanted to quit for a long time. Drinking does get old and feeling terrible each morning becomes torture, but the fear of not having the security blanket of a drink is much more terrifying than being without it. My body simply started to reject the alcohol. I got extremely bloated each time I drank. My system would not allow me to drink enough to get drunk. If I couldn't lose myself in the bottle or can...what was the use? I had reached my bottom. I was sick and tired of being sick and tired. I finally asked for help.

I remember what a relief it was to no longer be on the alcoholic merry-go-round. The days of planning my life around the drink were over. I was ready for a new life. I had to be open to change. I had to be open to listening to other people. No longer was I the master of the universe. For me to stay sober, I had to let God be in charge, and that, too, was a relief.

I, like many other addicts, are grateful for my bottom. It was a gift from God.

God, thank you for meeting me in the darkness of life. Set me free to love and serve you. Amen.

DEPENDING ON OTHERS

To the only God our savior, through Jesus Christ our Lord, belong glory, majesty, power, and authority, before all time, now and forever. Amen.
—Jude 1:25

Learning to take direction is one of the most important spiritual aspects of recovery. It is also the one that most new people struggle with. Our "best thinking" has got us into the depths of our addiction, but it is cannot get us out of it. We might think that if we just moderate our drinking or only drink on the weekends that we can still hang on; we won't lose control. Soon, though, we realize that moderate drinking is not the way of drinking that we enjoy.

My first sponsor was a man named Larry. He was a retired Baptist minister. He was old and cantankerous. I often did not like the way Larry shared his message, but it was usually the message I needed to hear. I want to be in recovery, but I also want to continue to do things my way. Having a sponsor in recovery forces us to follow someone else's direction and to see how asking for help is actually a gift. We are no longer alone in the world. We can depend upon other people for once (while keeping in mind that they are only human, too).

Today, I seek out other people's opinions and guidance. I know that I cannot live life alone. I need help from God and the people who know and care about me. Their words and wisdom are often a gift from God—if I am open to receiving them.

God, help me be open to you speaking to me through the lives of your people here on earth. Amen.

GRACE

*You are saved by God's grace because of your faith. This salvation is God's
gift. It's not something you possessed.*

—Ephesians 2:8

We addicts are famous for punishing ourselves. We will torture
ourselves day after day for everything we have done wrong and
all the hurt we have caused. We are relentless.

In recovery I experienced the gift of grace. As a United Methodist
pastor, I knew about grace; it is one of our theological cornerstones. We
had to understand it backward and forward for our ordination exams.
But, as we know, learning something from experience is much different
than reading about a concept in a book.

I realized, as I began to heal, that no matter what I had done, God
was still at my side. I was truly loved and accepted for who I was then
and who I am now. I did not have to get clean to be loved, nor do I now
have to do anything to keep God's love.

I took this experience to my congregation. I invited them to look at
the world through the lens of grace. Instead of having annual fundrais-
ers, what if we invited the community to our church and we gave everything away for free (just like grace)? Unfortunately, not everyone had
experienced God's grace as acutely as I had, and they were not ready to
share it so extravagantly. They, like me, were taught that we are to stand
on own feet; we are to earn what we need. I'm not saying that this sort
of attitude is wrong or bad, but I am glad this is not how God treats us.

We are loved by God no matter what we have done or how much
we believe we have failed. Nothing can separate us from the love of God.

◇◇

*God, thank you for your love and acceptance of me, just as I am.
Amen.*

◇◇

CHOICES MADE

Why do you see the splinter that's in your brother's or sister's eye, but don't notice the log in your own eye?

—Matthew 7:3

For most of my life, I hated my father. He was to blame for my wounding and, ultimately, my addiction. If only he had been able to accept me, to love me as I was, instead of terrorizing me, then I wouldn't have these problems.

I held on to this resentment for many years. I had prayed long and hard to forgive him. I actually thought I had, but then some new wound would pop up, and I would find myself hating him again.

My father passed away six months ago. I thought I would be relieved, but I wasn't. I was sad. Eventually, I came to accept that he was the way he was. He had good qualities and bad qualities. Ultimately, he was human.

I also realized that I had made my own choices. He did not force me to do drugs or alcohol. It was my decision. Would I have chosen a different path if I was raised in a loving home? Maybe. Maybe not. My dad is not to blame. Nobody is to blame. I chose to live as I did.

Today, I choose a different way. I am no longer a victim seeking pity for my rough life. I have experienced deep healing. I am enough. I am loved by God and by many. I would never suggest anyone go through what I did as a child, but I realize today that those scars allow me to care for others who are hurting. Everything in life can be a gift.

God, thank you for all of my life, good and bad. Show me the blessing and gifts in every day. Amen.

FREEDOM

But if we live in the light in the same way as he is in the light, we have fellowship with each other, and the blood of Jesus, his Son, cleanses us from every sin.

—*1 John 1:7*

I had been drinking like an alcoholic since I was sixteen. Every weekend involved binge drinking and blackouts. Since my mid-twenties I had quit a few times. Being a new Christian kept me sober for a couple of years, but after a while even my new love for Jesus would not keep me away from a drink.

I was thirty-five when I sat in a twelve-step meeting and said, "My name is Peter. I am an alcoholic." It was surreal to hear those words come out of my mouth. I had fought against that truth for many years. When I finally said those words, I was relieved. The truth was out.

Getting to that point was not as easy. I had physical complications due to my drinking. I had an angry wife and a restless church. But my biggest holdup was my image. I was a pastor of a major denomination. People would judge me. It would affect my career. Frankly, I was embarrassed.

But the truth also was that people were not at all surprised. Either they knew or suspected for a long time. My career actually improved because I was healthy. I did experience some judgment, but more importantly, I was now free from my secret. I did not realize how much energy I had put into hiding my addiction.

I walk today a free man. No secrets. I look the world in the eye and know God loves me.

God, thank you for taking me out of the darkness and into your light. Amen.

THE BIG BOOK

Your word is a lamp before my feet and a light for my journey.
—*Psalm 119:105*

The Big Book, *Alcoholics Anonymous*,[3] is the foundational text for alcoholics in 12-Step recovery. With its publication in 1939 a movement that began with two men, then three, has grown to include millions of people all over the world

The Big Book, as we call it, does not set down the scientific claims about alcoholism. It really is about one person, collaborating with other drunks, to tell their story about what life was like as an active alcoholic and what life is like in recovery. I find it fascinating that person after person has ordered the book. It's not unusual to hear someone say that they stayed up all night reading it or that they had to put it down because it hit too close to their own story. It also serves as a comfortable entry point. Some of us don't want to walk into a meeting facing a room full of strangers, but a book that we can read at our leisure is a good first step.

The main purpose of the book is for us, the reader, to have a spiritual experience. That we will find a God of our own understanding that will take away our obsession to drink or drug or eat or watch porn or overeat or under eat or cut or gamble or . . . There is a book for every 12-Step group. Interestingly, the focus of the book isn't addiction. It's God. God is always the answer.

Perhaps your next right step is ordering this book. If so, I hope you do it. I hope you will take the step after that and every step that follows. The road you are walking on leads to full life.

◇◇

God, thank you for offering me all I need to get sober and find recovery. Amen.

◇◇

ALLERGIES

People whose lives are based on selfishness think about selfish things, but people whose lives are based on the Spirit think about things that are related to the Spirit.

—Romans 8:5

The Big Book states that we who are alcoholics suffer from a phenomenon of mind and body that can be described as an allergy.[4] Whenever we take alcohol into our bodies it creates an allergic reaction that results in bodily craving and mental obsession. So, it says, we suffer from an obsession of mind and body, and no matter how long we go without a drink, once we take that first sip our allergic reaction begins immediately. For a long time, I resisted this notion. I could not believe that one sip would take me down that road again. I have since changed my mind.

My addiction to sugar ultimately convinced me. I love food. I always have. When it comes to sugar, my mind and body react differently than to any other food out there. Let's consider chocolate chip cookies. Specifically, let's think about Chick-fil-a chocolate chip cookies. I can go months without having one. But once I have one cookie, I want another. And another. Before I know it, I am gobbling down, Cookie Monster-style. But if I never had that first one, the mental and physical craving would never have been triggered. The monster would still be asleep.

All of my addictions function the same way. Once I start, I don't stop, and it takes a great amount of God's power to help me go one day without. I don't know why I am wired this way. The bottom line is that I am. I have to accept it. With God's grace I will stay sober today... to everything.

God, keep me from doing anything hurtful to myself today. Amen.

SPIRITUAL FITNESS

Therefore, stop worrying about tomorrow, because tomorrow will worry about itself.

—*Matthew 6:34*

I have spent most of my life with a victim mentality. My childhood was abusive, so I believe I deserve special treatment. You should not be mean to me or expect much from me because of my past. I also have anxiety about the future. When I am riding in an airplane, my thoughts are obsessed with when this plane is going to crash, because it is going to do so any minute, and I need to be ready. This focus on the past and fear of the future keeps me out of the present.

The recovery saying "one day at a time" invites me to look at my recovery from a realistic perspective. It does not matter how long I have been sober because I can relapse at any time. You will see people start to coast in their recovery and stop doing the things that keep them sober. They stop praying, going to meetings, and helping others. Before they know it, they are drinking or using again.

I have to keep spiritually fit. If not, my mind makes a beeline into the past or future. My mind also starts telling me lies. I begin to think that I exaggerated my drinking or using; it wasn't really *that* bad. I could handle it now. Lies. "Once an addict, always an addict," is true for me.

Today I am sober by God's grace. I have to seek God each day to help keep me sober.

My sobriety is contingent on my spiritual fitness. It may seem like work. It is. It is the work of healing.

God, help me keep my mind and heart centered on you. Amen.

DARKNESS

Some of the redeemed had been sitting in darkness and deep gloom; they were prisoners suffering in chains.

—Psalm 107:10

Many of us who struggle with addiction are also plagued by depression. It may be one reason our addiction started—we just wanted to feel better and our drug of choice numbed the pain. Unfortunately, addictions to substances like alcohol and sugar just make our depression worse.

Alcohol is a depressant. We may feel great while intoxicated, but once we sober up we crash. To restore those positive feelings, we have to drink even more; thus, the maddening cycle begins. Other substances and behaviors trigger the same cycle. The low after the high gets lower and lower.

Alcohol and other substances also interact with medications that many of us, including me, take to ease the depression. The medication works hard on my body chemistry to regulate my serotonin. When I was drinking, the effects of the alcohol were often at odds with the medication's effort, so the alcohol diminished the benefit I could have received from the medicine. I have found that total abstinence from alcohol is my only way out of the darkness of depression. By not drinking, I allow the medication to do its work.

I did not ask for depression. I need medication for my body to achieve chemical reactions it just does not complete on its own. I am past the days of feeling shameful for having to take medication. I now accept that I have depression. It really does not say anything about me as a person. I am not defective or weak; I just happened to be wired a certain way. I have discovered that telling the truth of my experience with depression can help others who suffer with it.

For me, drinking leads to depression. Surrendering the substances that keep us chained in the darkness is necessary if we are to walk in the light again.

God, remind me daily to surrender my life to you. Amen.

PRAYER

LORD, my God, listen to your servant's prayer and request, and hear the cry and prayer that I your servant pray to you.

—2 Chronicles 6:19

I learned about prayer in recovery. Previously, my prayers were always self-centered. I judged God and God's concern for me based on whether my prayers were answered the way I wanted them to be. If they weren't, I doubted God's existence, let alone God's love for me. But when life worked out in my favor, I believed God loved me, at least until I was let down again.

Many recovery groups recite the Lord's Prayer at the end of each meeting. I had grown up saying this prayer every Sunday. I knew it well. However, I never really paid attention to the words: "Thy will be done on Earth as it is in heaven." God's will be done. Not Peter's will be done.

My reintroduction to this prayer helped me begin to shift my focus from what I thought should be happening to what God was actually doing. Instead of trying to arrange life to suit me, I could open up and receive what life was offering, accepting both what I view as "good" and "bad" times of life. Distinguishing between "good" and "bad" times becomes harder when we consider how we have been shaped by those events we didn't welcome at first.

In recovery, our prayers become shorter. We give thanks to God for all things. We pray God's will, not ours be done. We begin seeking God for God's sake.

God, I pray your will be done. Amen.

CONFESSION

For this reason, confess your sins to each other and pray for each other so that you may be healed.

—James 5:16

One of the most valuable gifts of recovery is the opportunity to tell the truth, the whole truth, to someone we trust. It often comes in the fourth step when we list our resentments against persons, places, and things. This experience is a form of confession; it allows us to share all the anger, hurt, and fear that we have been carrying around in our heads and hearts and finally speak them out loud to someone who cares about us. No matter the structure of your recovery program, telling your truth and putting it into the light is necessary for healing.

Many would-be recovered addicts can't see this process through. It's terrifying. I understand. It was really scary for me. I remember making my list but leaving three things off. These three things would never be spoken of; I would take them to my grave.

The day came for me to sit down with my sponsor. He listened with patience and love. I got through all the items of my list. He thanked me and then started asking me questions. Then he asked me one final question: "Is there anything you have held back?"

The shameful secrets I had planned to keep came spilling out of me. I was scared, but the words kept coming. I finished; he gave me a loving smile and thanked me again, without judgement. He didn't even offer words of wisdom. Just grace. I felt so relieved. Finally, someone knew all of me and did not reject or abandon me. It was one of the greatest moments of my life.

God, you can have all of me good and bad. Thank you for your love. Amen.

A FALSE ME

When you search for me, yes, search for me with all your heart, you will find me.

—Jeremiah 29:13

Many of us who find ourselves in active addiction are really just looking for God. We are seeking intimate communion, acceptance, and security, which are all fruits of a relationship with God.

A relationship with God, however, is not always easy. It is an active endeavor that requires something from us, so we take the easier, softer way. We find a drug of choice that is accessible and (we think) under our control. We push the pump to receive more and more, and even though there are terrible consequences of our addiction, it is always waiting for us, eager to be reactivated. In a way, addiction is dependable.

I remember looking forward each day for my kids to fall asleep. As soon as they did, I would bring out my pipe to smoke weed. I loved how I felt high, like the world came alive and everything was more interesting. I had great ideas. I enjoyed life in those moments. And I believed I could live this way forever.

But then the drug would begin to wear off. A dullness, an emptiness, crept over me. I was disconnected from everything, including myself. I was still me, but not all of me. I had a vision of my soul being like a flower that was wilting. Each time I chose weed I lost something of myself, that self that was beautifully created by God.

Even so, it wasn't easy to set these false experiences aside and begin to seek the true God. Still today, I find myself wanting to turn back to that empty comfort instead of to God, believing that cheesecake, television, alcohol, or drugs will bring me fulfillment. They never do. I only find what I need in God.

God, let me find in you what I am trying to find in everything else.

YOU ARE ENOUGH

The righteous choose their friends carefully, but the way of the wicked leads them astray.

—Proverbs 12:26 (NIV)

Before recovery, I did not know how to be in relationship with another human being. I would try to use people who I thought could give me something. If I couldn't use someone, they had no value to me, and most often I would ignore them. People also scared me. I was afraid of their feelings and their judgement. I would work really hard to get people to like me; I felt safer when they did.

I continued to behave this way throughout my first few years of recovery. I would come late to the meetings and leave early. I was afraid people would talk to me and want something from me. I would be stuck either using people or taking responsibility for them. When I felt responsible for people, they became a burden, and I resented them. The truth is that they never asked me to take responsibility—I simply did not know how to interact as just me without taking or giving.

In the last few years, this pattern of interaction has shifted. I have developed deep friendships with people whom I see as equals. They have no value that I can manipulate nor do I need to take care of them. Each of us stands on our own yet provides care and the space to be our true selves.

This, I have discovered, was my deepest fear—being my true self. I felt like I was not enough, so I had to steal from you or care for you before you realize how disappointing I am. My outlook has changed. I know who I am. I am free from the need of anyone's validation. I am God's beloved child, and that is more than enough.

God, I am grateful for my relationship with you through Jesus Christ. Amen.

MAKING SPACE

But now I will heal and mend them. I will make them whole and bless them with an abundance of peace and security.
—*Jeremiah 33:6*

I spent a couple of years working in a treatment center for people who suffered from all types of addiction, including alcohol, drugs, codependence, sex/porn, and people with mood disorders like depression and anxiety.

Like most treatment facilities, we involved family members in therapy sessions. Often, a patient's spouse would have no idea that he or she was emotionally and spiritually affected by their loved one's addiction. They believed themselves perfectly healthy; if we could just please fix their loved ones, they believed, the family would be happy again.

Typically, what would follow was that the addict did get better but came home to a spouse who was still wounded and emotionally hurting. They were so accustomed to being in charge and taking care of the addict they no longer knew how to relate. The spouse, then, didn't even know what to do with a healthy loved one...which makes it hard for an addict to maintain recovery.

In order to give space to heal, family members need to allow the addict to function independently, even while maintaining whatever level of accountability is needed by both the addict and the loved one. The spouse can surrender their caretaking responsibilities and begin to let God care for their former addicts. They can begin caring for themselves and let others be responsible for their own lives.

This is not a simple or quick experience, though participation in a group like Al-Anon has helped many families. When you are used to taking care of other people, it can be difficult to take care of yourself without feeling guilty. Caring for ourselves is not selfish—in fact, it helps everyone, even the addict we love.

God, I surrender the people I love to you. Amen.

BEING WRONG—
AND ADMITTING IT

"Therefore, if you bring your gift to the altar and there remember that your brother or sister has something against you, leave your gift at the altar and go. First make things right with your brother or sister and then come back and offer your gift."

—Matthew 5:23-24

Addiction leaves a trail of chaos and hurt feelings. In recovery, we clean up the wreckage of our past, which usually includes saying, "I was wrong."

A lot of us drink or medicate because we want to forget the past, so facing those people and making amends is an important part of our healing process. We no longer have to numb our feelings or avoid the memories. Making amends allows us to redeem the past, allowing us to move forward as free people for today and the future.

In making amends, we say, "I was wrong," instead of, "I am sorry." The people we hurt are accustomed to empty promises and endless apologetic moments. After a time, they became immune to our words because nothing ever changed. We have to look people in the eye and take responsibility for our actions.

In most instances, people offer grace and forgiveness when you ask for them. But not always. People are still afraid of being hurt again. However, their reaction is not what is important. The key to our full recovery is cleaning up our side of the street.

For us to stay sober and enjoy this new life we have from God, we must admit we are human. We must admit we were wrong.

God, let me see where I was wrong and go to the people I have hurt.
Amen.

FINDING OURSELVES

On the day God created humanity, he made them to resemble God.
—Genesis 5:1

I n one of my journals from my early twenties I had written, "I want to become who God created me to be." If I have a personal mission statement, that is it. I had to change a lot in order for me to get there.

I had to get and stay sober. There is something about active addiction that takes us away from our heart and soul. We are not ourselves. We have lost our center. It takes us time to discover ourselves again. We may try on a lot of personas on the way to our true self. I had to engage different interests to see if they were a good fit. The path is crooked, but if we have the courage to continue to see the truth, we will find each day a clearer sense of "me."

In order to find the true self, we also have to be willing to let go of who we are not. Maybe people have tried to tell us what kind of person we are, or perhaps we had parents who tried to make us fit the mold they had for us. Even though these versions of ourselves never felt right, we kept them to make others happy and fulfill their expectations of us.

In recovery, we can no longer live to please others. We have to seek and be faithful to God only. This change can be scary. The people we have spent a lifetime pleasing will not be pleased by this change, and we fear they won't love us anymore. While giving space for their feelings, we must choose freedom over their expectations. We have to place God and the truth before all others. Only then will we come home to our true selves.

God, thank you for my sobriety and allowing me to discover the me you created. Amen.

FULFILLMENT

And so we know and rely on the love God has for us. God is love. Whoever lives in love lives in God, and God in them.

—1 John 4:16 (NIV)

Recovery helps us distinguish between essentials and distractions. In our addiction, we sought comfort and safety through our drug or behavior of choice. We isolated ourselves from our families and everyday life. When the window of sobriety opens up for us, we begin to view the world in a new light.

We see the things we have chased for so long are empty. We realize that we were never satiated by our addiction. No matter what our drug of choice was, it never fulfilled us. We went back to that empty well over and over believing this time it would fill us up, and it never did. That illusion was comforting, and we grieve its loss.

Our true fulfillment comes from God. God loves us perfectly, just as we are, right now, today. There is nothing we can do to change or deter God's love. Our job, then, is to accept God's love and offer it back to God. For some of us, like me, the experience of true and complete love is new. It is foreign, and accepting it takes practice. I seek to experience this gift through daily meditation.

Today, I crave God's love. Unlike the drugs and behaviors of my past, God's love does fulfill me and never runs out.

God, help me love you and receive your love through Jesus Christ. Amen.

FINDING YOUR WHY

*You teach me the way of life. In your presence is total celebration. Beautiful
things are always in your right hand.*

—*Psalm 16:11*

Addiction can be a slow form of suicide. Especially since many of us use our substances or behaviors to cope with underlying issues like depression, it's not unusual for an addict to hope their life will end. Any addiction is a form of self-harm; we turn to our behaviors and substances because living has become heavy.

I have been in that dark, dark place. While I never had a plan to kill myself, thoughts of it began creeping into my mind. A large part of me wanted to stay alive, but a smaller part was ready to let go. I reached out for help, and I strongly encourage you to do the same whenever thoughts or impulses to hurt yourself arise, even though it feels impossible. My spiritual mentor told me it is natural to have such thoughts. They are a sign that we are getting in touch with our deepest pain. He suggested that I set about figuring out both why I did not want to die and why I wanted to live.

I didn't want to die because I still believed then and now that God has a plan for my life. I love my family, and do not want to put them through the pain and grief that my death would cause.

Figuring out why I wanted to live was harder. I struggled with it for weeks before I had my answer. I won't share it here, not out of spite, but because I believe it's important that we all come to our own conclusion. There are no easy answers, and the process of working through the question is as important as the result.

Why do you want to live? Your answer may well determine the outcome of your recovery.

God, thank you for life. Help me find my "why." Amen.

NOTES

1. UNDERSTANDING & RECOGNIZING ADDICTION

1. *Diagnostic and Statistical Manual of Mental Disorders: DSM-5* (Arlington, VA: American Psychiatric Publishing, 2013), 585.

2 APPROACHES TO TREATMENT & RECOVERY

1. For more information, see Charlotte Davis Kasl, *Many Roads, One Journey: Moving Beyond the Twelve Steps (New York: Harper Perennial, 1992).*

2. For more information, visit www.celebraterecovery.com.

DEVOTIONS FOR YOUR JOURNEY THROUGH ADDICTION

1. For more information, see Melodie Beattie, *Codependent No More* (Hazeldon Foundation: Center City, Minnesota, 1992).

2. J. Luft and H. Ingham, "The Johari window, a graphic model of interpersonal awareness," Proceedings of the western training laboratory in group development (Los Angeles: University of California, Los Angeles, 1955).

3. Bill W., *Alcoholics Anonymous: The Story of How Many Thousands of Men and Women Have Recovered from Alcoholism* (New York: Alcoholics Anonymous World Services, 1976).

4. Ibid.